SPRUNG

Draper

ISBN: 978-1-915079-03-9

Cover designed by Aaron Kent

Edited and typeset by Aaron Kent

Broken Sleep Books Ltd
Rhydwen,
Talgarreg,
SA44 4HB
Wales

Contents

SPRUNG

Cai Draper

A Note on the Text

In late March 2020, around the time we entered the first lockdown, Mira put a call out on Twitter to ask if anyone would be interested in starting a poem-a-day project for April. Ellen and I responded. We set a few basic guidelines – that this would be a project of mutual support and encouragement, rather than feedback or criticism – and began the work. The poems in this book are taken, largely unedited, from that email chain. My deepest gratitude and respect to Ellen and Mira.

the period of daylight formerly known as Thursday

like a tortoise wrapped in blank verse

non-descript praise from the manager

panic uncovered in the corners

hooray

Hayley, Raymond, Stacey & Pottage

that's what I'd call my first four babies

born to a world of praise for the neighbours

delivery dude in a van in a zoo

registered nurse in a reified mask in a zoo

breathe in

life giving living to be filtering the toxins

breathe out

flush sing the savings to dash poison up the rafters

my sister six months pregnant & crying to the nursery

no midwife no baby group

no mum on the due date cursing

no big massive hug

the very expensive bath

scented everything scented birthplan centre of her

perennial thirst for learning

everything parallel everything universe everything muted

between us

cacophonic tones of the dream gaff in Clapton

I hope she is okay

we were remembering ourselves & my face is full of her

she can't see my face

write a poem on a tortoise

& blast it into space

2/4/20

we earned this

particular pinch of a Saturday

the minister breaking even from prediction

stick your very pointed brogues up Matthew

I'm glad there's no rest for the wicked

but may the beds of all workers feel perfect tonight

one takeaway

I have been organising my life around

white t-shirts on a weekday

another

piss in the bath was the triumph & joy

of a city boy's self-sufficiency

lemon balm & hyacinth

companionship

naivety

should you ever find me letting

go of my wide family

this is the recipe for my blood type

co-op

aunties

chips under ketchup

4/4/20

neighbourhood tired from banging the walls through

gold in the panes like talk of a windfall

the bedding is a tube map of circles

you are getting me to say what I hate most about you

my reluctance has the sneer of a secondary lover called Zack

you roll in dust forever then

all the colours of a classy thriller

go fishing

your bottom lip a goldmine

& finally it was time to make a picnic

said the tear-coloured bird to the worm in its beak

the witness was an imaginary child with real thumbs

what is not less significant

is the several rashes developed last fortnight

hanging off the stairs between us

6/4/20

stunning these days to wake

the question of how to draw for true parlance

floating

in the poetry

goldfinches busy as a series of sneezes

as for my mum I couldn't do the surprise

waxwork model on horseback rearing

it was too dangerous for the times

son

the window is thick with your lack of vision

so much of what we had to look forward to

bleeds itself out in the lines

at Tesco

son

am I grateful

for bumping into the couple who panic-ate and scarpered

for the lightness of my piss

for your life to exist

mum

yes as a question

what's clear is that I've been seeking the fullness of my taste

the growing ends & the maximum

as if the world spins on an axis

absurd

galactic

7/4/20

I will actually fight everybody

said the wrong manor cat to the rapper in the bath

literally all this neighbourhood is trying to build a pond

I hate cats said the rapper & stop talking like that

the cat sidled up & stuck his bum on a spindly

spiralling arm of the galaxy

demanded Dreamies

this poem is out of control said the rapper

be careful

it's starting to sound like something else

what happened to the pond

what happened to the fight

or the fact that the cat was in the wrong manor

& then I remembered everything

that was happening in the world

was happening inside my body

every second

in my living room

in our sexy times

dirt under my nails from the pond is full of it

sunlight through the lemon balm is full of it

the giant hole opening in the ozone layer

like a sideshow is full of it

the way it resembles a holiday

with a friend of a friend burning the breakfast

& thousands of people being killed by the government

8/4/20

I will put this growl

into upstart paper cuts for poster promotion

of a wild & ravishing dance in the sun

everyone's eggs in one basket

making unproductive love with danger

fuck forever

on the clock

or as long as the juice will allow

falling in love is not like falling through yet another trapdoor

it is too complicated

developing

understood by nothing but its own frameless portals

& even then

waney-edged

last night for the big words

as for the celebration

allow me & my friends the usual

hard drugs in name-tagged party bags

boundless city sex gardens plus

the nous to say interstices out loud

spaces the texture of our favourite resistance

revolution to suit the needs of a mood

where the dying of the wankers

is easy on the eye

& by the way

may the concept of Monday morning cease for A particularly

as for me

I'd like to go back in time & feature in the video for Wannabe

& hit David Cameron's weird lips with a pinger

fashioned from double-wrapped elastic band

cheap red balloon & blue raspberry Panda Pops bottle

fuck David Cameron particularly

those Chelsea boots really did my nut

I wonder who he'd love when fleeing

but more than anything

I want to take MDMA with my mum

& listen to Everything But the Girl

& have the most luxurious comedown

where doom is just a random word

folks use for backwards mood

in the morning the neighbours congratulate us on our bedtime

bring us the perfect eggs or not eggs

telepathy is real

for the duration of the afternoon we walk through the summer

on the sofa in our minds

& bump into a few exes

give them thanks for their words & choices

discuss it afterwards on a dappled veranda

tropical flavour Lucozade in the fountain

as the evening draws in

the dead pets rise from their graves

under the crab apple tree

shudder off the mulchy sleep

& after a convivial catch up deliver us

a shameless household classic

a capella

while filling our lungs with compost

breathing for us

they plant us

bulbs

in bed

the rabbits tap a lavish BPM

we know this to be primordial

the one that lives before & after

they are pulling the earth back over

catching our light through the grains of sand

that pock the turf like stars

9/4/20

I am sort of work clothes gently

fraying as the body soaks in

a whole way of sitting down

see me done by breakfast

a flying disc in the park of my trousers

flag down half all the deep dark day

I've been gone & unfriendly

now is the game of returning to work

lying to my boss about start time & invite

derivative

signature

end game

ligaments

being from a family of therapists

I clock my own makeup in seconds split

to recognise the difficult text of an aunt

is what isn't fully in poetry

the lipstick spins out the tube

quotidian

the button drawn out

the belly of condition & into concrete expression

fuck metaphysics & guess what

I am Kate Nash in the gloaming

I am Toadfish from Neighbours in roadkill form

the future manifests from memory

says Kanye

I believe him

16/4/20

as in in

as in spire

as in going through the roof at god

I have a strong desire to invent the history of the spanner

knowing nothing would be better if certain people weren't

begging to die for capitalism

when a ring changes finger

the finger feels a hunger akin to shadowless noon

finger

as in fing

as in er

 as in engross yourself in the pluck of disgust

I used to work with a kid who'd attack then scream

I hate myself at the top of his lungs

his teacher was a Spaniard with pointy beard & bandy legs

who made the most delicious tortilla

Spaniard

as in span

as in yard

as in rove the lengths of your garden like an empire

Christopher Columbus had a strawberry mark

in the shape of America

on the inside of his eyelid

this is what made him sleep red

mania

as in main

as in ear

as in the bellicose framing of audio

I tell my niece what is amazing about writing

is it's yours to do what you will with

& wonder how white that is

everybody understands better than white people

that white people need to understand themselves better

at the wedding in Marrakech

when Noor said to us

of course the white people are early

we regarded each other curiously

& almost as if we'd been practising our whole lives

said in unison

I have literally no idea what you're talking about

17/4/20

brewing is a thing that isn't tea

it is the call to stringing up your arteries

round London like bunting

as to eat the fry up

is to pine for a podcast of silence & lie you can chat

get pre-loved hype from another gaff

the butcher is having a field day

bang bang

smash the sausages

axe the eggs

fling the beans into oblivion

I'm acting progression through the fact of caring

about clichés about work

I do everything I'm told

oh look

what a beautiful screen

the crème eggs the neighbours drop round are pressurised

eek

out a little gas on the chomp

at which we turn our earshells inward

too many people are

dying

insects curling

strew the filling pond bottom

I am trying more than ever to stop saying I am

but I am failing & I am

not understanding the imperative

but it do

as the streak to learn the Norfolk ways do too

what would it mean to be a Tetris part that droops

itself to fitting ill

the parts of the sliding doors where the paint's crud aft

are sending me

part airhead part ingrate sounding off

there is a clouded reason

nerves

ride the gravy train through the body whole

to the gravy add powdered blood & start living

it's better than the other thing

so the laptop gets ordered from Argos in bed

& the rush is a sprouting bean

& I am a boy & my name is Jack

& up & up I go

& fee

& fie

& foe

the view is six green kids inside a giant Corsa bro

18/4/20

one of the main problems with being alive

is that other people accept you more than yourself

this specific thing makes me go into the corner

& bang my head

it's okay Cai they say

but stop banging your head

& I say what you really mean when you say that

is you want me to bang my head even harder

if you didn't then you wouldn't have said the opposite

that's when they look baffled & upset

& say I don't understand come & sit with me

okay

then we hug but it doesn't feel like a hug should

it feels like a very bad piece of wood forever

there's a mosquito rubbing itself into the living room window

in the evening sun

mostly what I contemplate

is where the next headswoon is coming from

& by that I don't mean weed or wine

but perhaps the swan

bossing its way through Venice now the boats've gone

22/4/20

navigating the comma

navigating the navel

inner

linten

portal

sometimes I tickle myself & come out egged in Manchester

circa two thousand & nine

today I am grateful for the lack of egging

& the fact of no weed left

I smoked it all in a kissing gate feeling absurd as I said

I am trying to say exactly what I mean

the windows remain

very dirty

I am scared I will never be able to live with another person again

this morning I have already had three arguments

one with my boss about the spreadsheet

one with my neighbour about British Summer Time

one with myself about the way the first two were dealt with

for each of them I was completely alone

for a good portion of the time

my thoughts resemble giant hairy caterpillars not born of me

M says not every deviation is betrayal

so big up the moments of divine junk

sometimes I stick my hand through my belly button

& come out washing rocket

down the basement kitchen in New Cross

sturdily booted Arriva Jesus flailing greased apron & busted pot

dancing with a broom like Turbo in Wildstyle

without recourse to clear fishing lines holding it up

saying that

I did know a man who walked the New Cross Road barefoot

& came back to life after an accident

which cured him of his taste

but not his thirst

30/4/20

today I would like to encourage the sky to dance about my head

wind blowing concrete

thick chancer down thoroughfare

then question what drip comprising the firmament

rubs the noise whitely & static blurred in

the first chapter of a book called the Star Maker

took me sixteen years to read

in every sentence bitter tastes

the feasibility of moving worlds

away from the body through space

once I blamed being a prick on reading too much

sci fi with a straight face

this is the closest the world has ever seemed to closing down

yet here we are

dipping our poems in chocolate sauce & sniffing

fingertips like it's a genuine weekend

& not any new slick grey arrow

hurling itself out our throat towards bedtime

2/5/20

I would write in praise of walking

if the joggers didn't rhyme with themselves in my face

follow the vector to cumulus high

culminating greys of a bilious

staunch & stubborn sky

the inscrutable seated of Norwich

land of chair

closed as a library

sniffing on each sill's stickiness

is a step in the direction of you

my city

but I ain't stirring this morning

I am eating an apple & mooching

to stay put a lot makes my bellies

throw a petty fist in the dungeon

about time we got going

said the moonwalking ghost to the flesh in its den

has the concept of structural forwardness

shut up shop

its trap

or what

coz I don't know road from ant track from flight path

from pipework from flume from stinking landfill rivulet

now that B&Q is open

woohoo

does the Mountain of Shit feel relief or dread

do egrets feel breeze to be cleaner these days

or the cormorant calmer in firmament

roaming

a case of inside the horizon

at the back of the pub where the taps are still working

I chat a bunch & outstay my welcome

3/5/20

in the Dolores Umbridge of existences

desire to commune approximates blue curds lapped at

in the moonlight

washed in smudge & thinnest pigment

crossing crass grasses to a Vauxhall Corsa always

somehow even more so with the sock & tarmac tip toe

twenty thousand pennies up a morsel

forgive me

this lacks as much as such is me to live with

lemon balm destroyed by imposter

I squirm at the name of justice

a thing from a whole nother household

no wonder

a patent lack of tasks leaves me gagging at the roaches

as for the here & now

if this fly continues its business

I am liable to do something I hold value against

namely

imagine getting killed by a rich & lazy giant

not that the fly may be glory seeking

but if it is

read it Defoe's account of the 1665 sickness

smoke so much weed emails resemble a papier maché

punch bowl in a post-encounter hedge

& invite the fly to Valhalla

the rain seeping through like malware

4/5/20

today's the day I release the photos of my burial mound

made of disposable lighters pilfered from the artist

nervous at the doors to the space

lighters

& a sheaf of part stuck collages

lighters

collages

& a Friday night of half cut colleagues whipping themselves

into soft peaks

this morning I found a pair of Oreo doughnuts in a box

with a see through top

perched on a gate post at the front of my house

I took them in immediately

it was too dangerous

5/5/20

in continued consternation

my main question is could I burn myself raw

onto a tape of the Spice Girls

when we say we're being called to by an inanimate object

does that mean like flippant burner call or

scheduled DMC

a wise man once told me it's better to focus on the how

than the what

actually it wasn't a wise man

it was a house track in a club

o

herd

I hear

caveats at eleven forty seven

I think I am interested in the avant garde

in the same way I wanted to slow dance with Emma

at the year seven ball

dizzying prospect in a privately rented hall

I read the words avant garde & my heart feels excellent

like that Jeremy Deller film of the washing machine

flinging off the centrifugal innings of itself

nothing makes the sentence the avant garde's in make sense

like red leaves or the concept of de-arrest

button me holy I'm covered I'm holding on fast

9/5/20

today it was explained to me that dandelion means lion's teeth

I was like woah cool

how much dandy foraging am I actually willing to do

keeping a packed lunch of puffballs

a very vague intention

like the vague

A11

vague body of a mammal red across the A11

vague petrol gauge in the go kart

vague hour & buzz in the membrane

indicator

vague

of tension

vague hair do

vague birthday

since when did numbers telescope

birds eye view of a pinprick stovepipe

pinched at the finish of the sightline

eureka

I've had Four Weddings and a Funeral

Jurassic Park & Rush Hour 2

on in the background for four lots of eight years

my favourite outtake was damn

he ain't gonna be in Rush Hour 3

oh that

oh

I have my fingers in my ears

11/5/20

Fred Seidel says too much is not enough

Chris Tucker says follow the rich white man

I say I'm high all the time which is both

double rainbow guy didn't need drugs

he just needed a double rainbow

RIP double rainbow guy

RIP Ty

no-one ever really dies

someone said Piers Morgan

shouting at the Tory MP on the TV made him cry

I don't know what to think but the magnesium

a poem made from stardust burns in the dark

nooks of a padlocked academy

it was lit by the ghost of the teacher who marked so many

essays one Sunday

their entire body was repurposed

for the automatic door in the sky

12/5/20

today I have mostly been thinking sideways from between

you & me

a massive bowl of clams speaking in funding applications

electronics in the sonic sea

the ways I rode to you were a whole next B road

birds were coming up & my love they still are

to write about the hovering pause

at the prospect of cooking for one as it feels

like a poet at the start of a novel

or the delicate crust of mortar skirting bricks outside my window

its watery crest & spray

breaking on the sandbank off Yarmouth

15/5/20

Notes on the poems

2/4/20: this poem is for Sian.

9/4/20: this poem is for my mum.

17/4/20: this poem is for Noor & Mustapha.

18/4/20: this poem is for Hannah & Jimmy (thanks for the crème eggs).

30/4/20: the line 'not every deviation is betrayal' is from Mira Mattar's poem 'The Light of Day is Sweet to the Eyes'.

15/5/20: this poem is for Lotte.

Acknowledgements

A big thank you to the editors of the following magazines and journals who published earlier versions of these poems: Anthropocene, Babel Tower Notice Board, Spontaneous Poetics, Lucky Pierre, PERVERSE, Seiren, No Contact, Milly and Erotoplasty.

LAY OUT YOUR UNREST